Science Skills

5

Pupil's Book

by

Jocelyne Churchill

CAMBRIDGE
UNIVERSITY PRESS

SCIENCE SKILLS 5

Contents

Projects and experiments	Documentaries
• Make a *Book of life* • Discover why plants have a cell wall	• Living or non-living?
• Do a presentation on an ecosystem • Investigate how animals survive the cold of the Arctic tundra	• Amazing adaptations
• Create and promote your own nature reserve • Find out the best way to clean up an oil spill	• Cooperation is key
• Create a plan to save energy at home • Discover how important light is for plants	• Shine on sunny sun
• Design a campaign warning about the risks of too much energy • Investigate how sound travels and why telephones used to have cords	• Hear energy, see energy, feel energy
• Design and build a light-up board game • Find out what happens when you change components in an electrical circuit	• Electricity everywhere

Extra activities  Page 90

WHAT IS NATURAL SCIENCE?

Science helps us understand how the world works. It helps us solve problems and can make life easier.

How are the people in the photos using science?

Look around you. Where is science being used?

 Which photo is being described? Listen and guess.

Do you ever wonder how something works, why something happens or how changing something would make a difference? Scientists use the **scientific method** to understand the world around us. It always starts with a **question**.

I wonder why / how ...?

How does ... work?

What would happen if ...?

Scientists then decide how to answer the question by thinking of an **experiment**. Before carrying out the experiment, they guess what will happen. This guess is called a **prediction** or a **hypothesis**.

Scientists draw **conclusions** from their observations and the **results** of their experiments. These conclusions help us to understand the world we live in.

1 LIVING THINGS

Look and discuss...

Which kingdom is each organism from?
Which kingdom is missing?

Life has done extremely well here on Earth. Scientists estimate several million species live on our planet!

I think this organism belongs to ...

Yes, I think so, too. / I'm not sure about that.

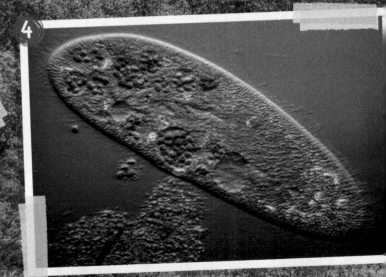

Plant 1, 7; Animal 2, 8, 6;
Fungus 3, 5; Protist 4, 6;
missing kingdom: Monera

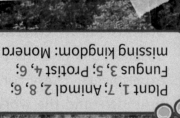

6

5

6

7

8

Can you name the seven characteristics of living things?

Explore

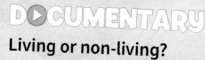

Make a *Book of Life*. You will:

- learn about different types of cells.
- research information and take notes about an interesting organism.
- organise facts and share information with others.
- present the information you have collected.

WHAT ARE CELLS MADE UP OF?

All living things are made up of **cells**. Although we can only see them with a microscope, they are very important.

Discover...

what the jelly-like substance inside a cell is called.

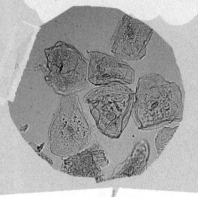
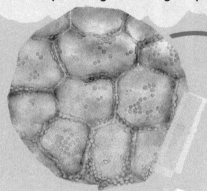

The cells on the far left are human cheek cells. Can you guess what type of organism these cells belong to?

Cells may look very different from one another, but they have got several similar characteristics and structures.

1 Nucleus: controls what happens inside the cell and contains all the genetic information.

2 Cytoplasm: jelly-like substance which helps give the cell shape and is where all the cell structures are found.

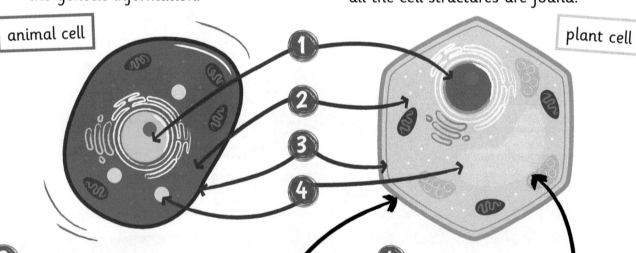

animal cell

plant cell

3 Cell membrane: controls the movement of substances in and out of cells.

Cell wall: gives structural support to the cell.

4 Vacuole: a storage space for the cell.

Chloroplasts: help the plant make food from sunlight and water.

Find out about other structures within a cell. What jobs do they do?

WHY HAVE PLANT CELLS GOT A RIGID WALL?

Discover...

the differences between plant and animal cells.

Background: There are some similar structures in animal and plant cells, but only plant cells have got a cell wall.

Hypothesis: Why have plants cells got a cell wall? Write your hypothesis in your notebook.

Materials: eight balloons, four shoe boxes

Step 1: Blow up the balloons (not too big). Put one balloon in each shoe box and leave the rest out.

Step 2: Build two towers, one using only the balloons and the other using the shoe boxes with balloons inside.

Reflect ❶

What do the balloons represent?
What do the shoe boxes represent?

Reflect ❷

Which tower is easiest to build?

Conclusion: What is the function of a plant cell wall?

Cell walls provide ...

Animal cells haven't got a cell wall. Compare the human body with a tree. What has the human body got to help with support that a tree hasn't?

The human body has got ... , whereas a tree ...

HOW DO CELLS COMBINE TO MAKE BIGGER THINGS?

Cells are the structural units of life, but their function doesn't stop there!

cell

Can you name any of the systems in the human body?

system

Organs work together to make **systems**.

What organs are in a plant?

tissue

Most cells work with other similar cells to make layers, known as **tissues**. For example, individual muscle cells combine to form muscle tissue.

organ

Many tissues work together to make **organs**, like the heart, skin or stomach. Each organ has got a specific job.

What is the biggest muscle in the human body?

organism

All the systems work together to ensure that we function properly as an **organism**. Other organisms, such as animals, plants and fungi have got the same organisation. Only the basic structural units — the cells — are different from ours.

Some organisms, such as bacteria, are **unicellular**. They have got one cell that does everything.

What do you call an organism with many cells?

Explore STAGE 1

- Choose an interesting organism.
- Find out if it is unicellular or multicellular. Investigate what types of cells, tissues, organs or systems it has got.
- Draw the organism on a piece of paper and add labels.

WHICH KINGDOM DO YOU NEED A MICROSCOPE TO SEE?

Discover...

which kingdoms contain both unicellular and multicellular organisms.

Scientists classify all living things into **five kingdoms**.

Protists come in many different shapes and sizes. Some protists take in food, like this **unicellular** protozoon. ▶

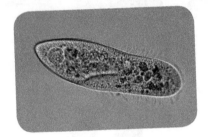

◀ Other protists are **multicellular** and make their own food, like this giant kelp, which is an alga.

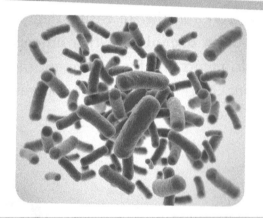

◀ Bacteria are in the **Monera** kingdom and are unicellular. They are so tiny that you need a microscope to see them. Most bacteria get their nutrition from other organisms.

Investigate how many types of bacteria have been found in the human tummy button.

Plants are multicellular. They make their own food from sunlight and water. ▶

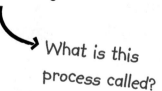

What is this process called?

▼ Many people think fungi are plants, but they're wrong! **Fungi** cannot make their own food, so they must break down other organisms to get energy. Most fungi are multicellular.

Find out what unicellular fungi are called.

▼ **Animals** are multicellular. Like fungi, they cannot make their own food. The two main groups of animals are **vertebrates** and **invertebrates**.

Which vertebrate or invertebrate sub-groups do these animals belong to?

STAGE 2

- **Find out more about the organism you chose in Stage 1.**
- **How does it obtain nutrients? How does it move? How does it reproduce? Which kingdom does it belong to?**
- **Write the information in bullet points.**

🎧 Listen to Katie and Matt talking about three different organisms. Write down the characteristics and then classify each organism into a kingdom.

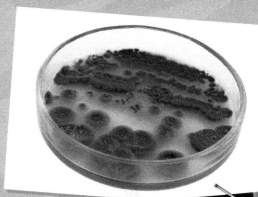

Although bacteria can be helpful to humans, they also cause disease. Alexander Fleming discovered that certain fungi produce a substance called penicillin, which kills dangerous bacteria. Many lives have been saved or improved since the discovery of this first **antibiotic**.

Have you ever had to take antibiotics?

WHAT DOES DICHOTOMOUS MEAN?

Discover...

what scientists use dichotomous keys for.

Dichotomous means *divided into two*. Scientists use **dichotomous keys** to identify organisms they find in the wild. All the characteristics defined in a dichotomous key have two choices. For example, living or non-living.

You can build a dichotomous key to identify organisms based on nutrition, number of cells or what they look like.

Look back

How do we know if something is living or non-living?

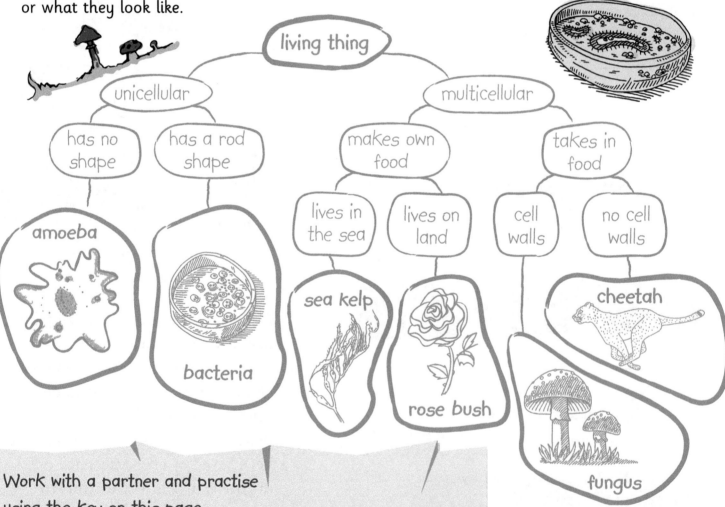

living thing

unicellular

has no shape

has a rod shape

amoeba

bacteria

multicellular

makes own food

lives in the sea

lives on land

sea kelp

rose bush

takes in food

cell walls

no cell walls

cheetah

fungus

Work with a partner and practise using the key on this page.

It's multicellular and makes its own food.

It lives in the sea.

It must be sea kelp.

Now make your own dichotomous key using different organisms!

CAN YOU CLASSIFY THESE WEIRD AND WONDERFUL ORGANISMS?

Discover...

which plant gets its food by eating other living things.

Like all rules, exceptions exist. Some organisms are tricky to classify!

The platypus lays eggs, but is not a reptile, fish or bird.

How is the platypus classified?

The Venus flytrap is no ordinary plant – it gets its energy by eating insects! However, it can still make its own food between meals like other plants.

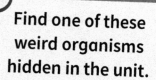

Find one of these weird organisms hidden in the unit.

This may look like a plant, but it is actually a leaf-tailed gecko. It can mimic leaves to avoid being eaten.

This looks like a tree, but it is actually a marine animal called *Spirobranchus giganteus*, known as the *Christmas tree worm*. The tentacles are actually specialised mouths!

This lichen gives taxonomists a double headache. It is both a fungus and an alga living together in the same organism.

What is a taxonomist?

Explore   STAGE 3

- Find out three interesting facts about your organism.
- Swap information with a partner. Which organism is the strangest?
- Make a poster of your organism. Include your drawing and information from Stages 1 and 2.
- Add photos and write a descriptive paragraph about your interesting facts.

Check this out: ...

Can you believe that ...?

Believe it or not, my organism has got / does / is / can ...

15

1 Match the prefixes to the endings. Complete the sentences in your notebook.

Prefixes: uni- multi- in- anti- -cellular -biotics -vertebrates -cellular

a An organism that contains several different cells that work together is a ..... organism.

b Bacteria have only got one cell and are an example of a ..... organism.

c There are two main groups of animals: vertebrates and ..... .

d Sally is feeling better because the ..... she is taking are fighting her bacterial infection.

2 Write the correct question word. Match each question to the correct answer.

a ..... does giant kelp grow?

b ..... have plant cells got a cell wall?

c ..... discovered penicillin?

d ..... kingdom does the platypus belong to?

e ..... do plants make their own food?

f ..... is the plural of *fungus*?

Fungi.
Through photosynthesis.
For structural support.
Alexander Fleming.
In the sea.
The Animal kingdom.

3 Complete the sentences using the modal verbs *must* or *might*.

a This organism is unicellular, but doesn't make its own food; it ..... be a bacterium.

b This organism is unicellular and makes its own food; it ..... be a protist.

c This organism is multicellular with cell walls; it ..... be a fungus.

d This organism is multicellular and makes its own food; it ..... be a plant.

e This organism is a multicellular vertebrate; it ..... be an animal.

1 For these questions, choose the correct answer for each gap.

a ..... are the building blocks of life.

Kingdoms   Organs   Cells

✓ Assessment link
For more Unit 1 activities go to page 78.

b Tissues work together to form ..... .

organisms   systems   organs

c ..... look like plants but they can't make their own food.

Protists   Bacteria   Fungi

d The ..... controls the cell and contains all the genetic information.

nucleus   cytoplasm   chloroplast

2 Copy and complete the mind map.

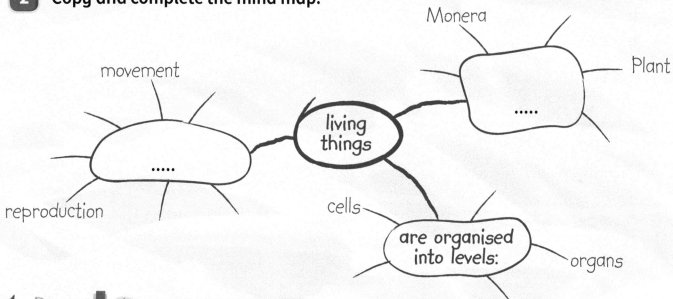

Explore   FINALE

- Get into expert groups for each kingdom. Discuss what your organisms have in common. Are they all multicellular? Do they make their own food?

- Now form new groups of five, each person representing a different kingdom. Talk about your organism and present your poster.

- Your teacher will then collect the organism posters and organise them into a book: *The Book of Life!*

I have chosen ... because ...

This is an organism that can / does / is ...

2 ECOSYSTEMS

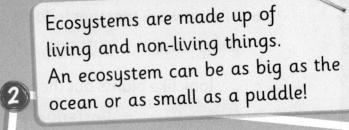

Ecosystems are made up of living and non-living things. An ecosystem can be as big as the ocean or as small as a puddle!

Look and discuss...

Can you name these ecosystems?

I think this ecosystem is a ...

I'm not sure. It looks more like a ...

1 grassland; 2 desert; 3 freshwater;
4 forest; 5 marine; 6 urban; 7 tundra

5

6

S☁ng
Ecosystems on Earth

How are the ecosystems similar?
How are they different?

7

D►CUMENTARY
Amazing adaptations

Explore

Explore an ecosystem from a different continent and do a presentation. You will:

• discover the characteristics of an ecosystem.

• learn about different types of ecosystems.

• find out how animals adapt to their surroundings.

WHAT MAKES UP AN ECOSYSTEM?

Discover...

the difference between a population and a community.

sunlight

air quality

temperature

climate

rocks

water

soil

The **non-living** components of an ecosystem are called the **abiotic factors**.

An **ecosystem** is made up of a **community** of **living things** and the **physical environment** that surrounds them. The living things that make up the community can be from any of the five kingdoms.

What are the living components of an ecosystem known as?

Look back...

Can you remember the names of the five kingdoms?

A **habitat** is the home of a living thing. The habitat of the endangered Iberian lynx is the grassland in the south of Spain.

individual

A group of the same **individual** is called a **population**. Different populations that interact with each other are called a **community**.

population

community

Living things in an ecosystem are divided into two main groups: **flora** (plants) and **fauna** (animals).

Explore STAGE 1

- Choose one of the following ecosystems: the Atacama Desert, the Great Barrier Reef, the Amazon Rainforest, New York City or the Serengeti National Park.
- Research the living and non-living components of your chosen ecosystem.

WHAT IS A SAVANNAH?

Discover...
the different types of grassland.

Grasslands are large areas of grass, found in places with very little rain. Trees need a lot of rain to grow which means that grass and small plants tend to grow instead.

Savannahs are found in tropical areas where there is more rain. For this reason, you may see some trees, but not many! Elephants, giraffes and zebras live here.

Temperate grasslands are found in cool climates, normally where it is dry and windy. The grass is often shorter. Bison, deer, wolves and rabbits live here.

Do you know what the word *temperate* means? Find out!

A male lynx needs to eat one rabbit per day to survive. If you had to eat only one thing a day, what would it be?

 Listen to Hannah. What type of ecosystem did she visit? What animals did she see?

The Iberian lynx lives in the grasslands of Spain. The thick grass provides shelter and the open land makes it easy to hunt rabbits.

WHERE DO BROWN BEARS LIVE?

Rainy places allow trees to grow in large groups known as **forests**.

Coniferous forests are located in the colder zones of the northern hemisphere. Brown bears, reindeer, moose, wolves and weasels live among evergreen trees.

Deciduous forests are dominated by trees whose leaves change colour and fall off each autumn. You can find deer, squirrels, beavers, foxes and wild boar here.

We can find over half the plant and animal species on Earth in **tropical rainforests**. Located near the equator, the temperature is high, but there is lots of rain.

Like their name suggests, **Mediterranean forests** are found near the Mediterranean Sea. Typical flora includes oak trees, rosemary and thyme.

STAGE 2

- **Find out about the climate and location of your chosen ecosystem.**
- **Make a spider diagram showing the information you have found out so far.**

living things   non-living things

Amazon Rainforest

location   climate

HOW DO CAMELS SURVIVE IN THE DESERT?

Discover...

how organisms have adapted to high temperatures and little water.

Deserts are the hottest and driest places on Earth. During the day, temperatures can reach up to 50 °C, but can drop to 0 °C at night. Living things have adapted to the changes in temperature and the lack of water.

What is the largest desert in the world? Where is it found?

When it is scorching hot outside, what better way to beat the heat than to sleep all day? Many desert animals are **nocturnal**. They are only active at night when it is cooler.

Find examples of nocturnal animals.

A cactus can **store water** for long periods of time. They have got a thick waxy layer and **spines** instead of leaves, which reduces water loss. The spines also protect the cactus from animals that might want to eat it!

Camels **store nutrients** in their humps and lose hardly any water through sweating or urination. This means they can go for a long time without having a drink or a snack!

Explore STAGE 3

- **Research the flora and fauna of your ecosystem.**
  What are the adaptations needed to live in this ecosystem?
  Think about food, water, predators, prey and climate.

- **Add the information to your diagram from Stage 2.**

- **Tell a partner what you discovered.**

I found out that ...

I discovered that ...

WHY DO POLAR BEARS NEED TO BE FAT?

Discover...

how some animals can survive in very cold temperatures.

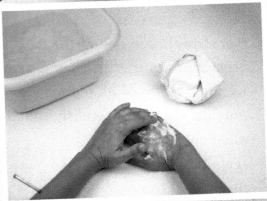

Background: Some animals that live in very cold temperatures have got a thick layer of fat, called blubber.

Hypothesis: If you had more fat on your body, would you notice the cold as much? Why? / Why not?

Materials: large bowl, water, ice cubes, butter

Step 1: Get a bowl large enough to fit both hands in. Fill it with water and ice cubes. Leave it for five minutes.

Step 2: Put both hands in the bowl and count to ten. Take your hands out and warm them for a few minutes. This is the **control**.

Step 3: Now, rub butter over one hand. Put both hands back in the water and count to ten.

Step 4: Wash your hands with warm water and soap.

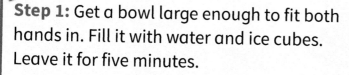

Reflect ①

How does each hand feel in the water? Do both hands feel the same?

Reflect ②

How does each hand feel this time? Do both hands feel the same?

In conclusion, ...

Conclusion: What did you find out? Do you think extra fat on your body would keep you warmer? Why?

Animals in colder climates need ...

WHAT LIVES IN A POND?

Discover...

the difference between a marine and a freshwater ecosystem.

Aquatic ecosystems can be ...

MARINE

Water type: salt water
Examples: oceans and seas
Flora: giant kelp, seagrass, sea grapes and plankton
Fauna: sharks, turtles, dolphins, crabs, jellyfish and sponges
Fact: It is the largest ecosystem on Earth!

FRESHWATER

Water type: fresh water
Examples: lakes, rivers, streams and ponds
Flora: bulrushes, reeds and waterlilies
Fauna: fish, crocodiles, turtles and frogs
Fact: Water is constantly recycled.

Coral reefs are one of the most diverse ecosystems on Earth. They are home to about 25% of all marine life. Many animals, such as clownfish, sponges and sea anemones make coral reefs their home because of the safety they provide.

Find a marine reptile hidden in the unit.

Despite their small size, **ponds** are home to a variety of aquatic life, like snails, frogs, fish and large birds, such as herons.

The **shoreline** is where the sea meets the land. Organisms that live here, such as starfish, molluscs and sea urchins, have adapted to strong tides and waves. Most can stick to the surface of rocks.

Protists dominate aquatic ecosystems. Are protists unicellular or multicellular?

WHICH BIRD OF PREY LIVES IN NEW YORK CITY?

Instead of adapting to ecosystems, humans have adapted ecosystems to suit them. These are known as **urban ecosystems**. They have got many **artificial elements**, but also contain **natural elements**.

Discover...

the natural and artificial elements of an urban ecosystem.

Artificial elements include buildings, airports, parks and bridges.

What are the natural elements of an urban ecosystem? Discuss.

The natural elements include ...

Animals can survive here because ...

New York City has got a higher **peregrine falcon** population than most places on Earth. All the skyscrapers make a great habitat for these birds of prey. They provide an ideal look-out point, in the same way cliffs do, for prey such as pigeons and blackbirds.

Explore   STAGE 4

- Now that you have studied the different types of ecosystem, you can add this information to your diagram. What characteristics define your chosen ecosystem?

- Does your ecosystem contain any artificial elements? Find out and make a list of the consequences of human interference.

1 Complete the sentences in your notebook with the correct form of the adjective or adverb.

a The spines on a cactus make it ..... (good) at reducing water loss than a plant with broad leaves.

b Tropical rainforests are home to a ..... (diverse) range of species than anywhere else in the world.

c Temperatures in temperate grasslands are ..... (extreme) than in deserts.

d The Iberian lynx can hunt ..... (effective) in a habitat with thick grass and open land than in a city.

e Thanks to their blubber, polar bears and seals can tolerate cold temperatures ..... (easy) than most other animals.

2 Look at the photos. Talk with a partner about urban ecosystems. Mention the things in the box.

> natural elements   artificial elements   habitats
> habitat destruction   pollution   air quality

Also, …

What's more, …

However, …

On the other hand, …

3 Do you prefer urban or rural environments? Discuss with a partner.

1 Unscramble the letters to make words. Use some of the words to complete the sentences.

Assessment link
For more Unit 2 activities go to page 80.

eceosstmy   svaahnsna   dpaat   oulpoatipn   htbaiat   sderte

a ..... are a type of grassland found in tropical areas.
b A ..... is the home of a living thing.
c An ..... is made up of a community of organisms and the abiotic factors in an area.
d Living things ..... to their natural surroundings.

2 Look at the photos and identify the ecosystems. Write down two characteristics of each ecosystem.

 **FINALE**

- Prepare and carry out a presentation on your ecosystem. You can find others who have chosen the same ecosystem and work in pairs or small groups.

- Use the information you have collected and include some pictures or videos.

- Think about the structure of your presentation. How many sections will it have? What are you going to say? What is your partner going to say?

THE BIOSPHERE

The biosphere is the sum of all the ecosystems on Earth. These ecosystems form an enormous puzzle. If there is a piece missing in the puzzle, the rest of the biosphere is affected.

Look and discuss...

Which living things in the photos are cooperating? Which are competing?

These living things are cooperating by ...

... and ... are competing for food / shelter / resources.

cooperating 1, 3, 4, 5, 7; competing 2, 6, 8

5

6

Song
Biodiversity

Apart from cooperation and competition, what other ways do living things interact?

8

7

DOCUMENTARY
Cooperation is key

Explore

Create your own nature reserve and make a website, leaflet or poster to promote it.

You will:

- learn how living things interact.
- discover how humans can negatively affect the habitats of other species.
- find out why it is important to protect species' habitats.
- learn about nature reserves.

WHAT ARE THE DIFFERENT PARTS OF A FOOD CHAIN?

All living things need energy. A **food chain** shows us how energy passes between organisms in an ecosystem.

Discover...

how organisms get the energy they need.

sun

All food chains start with the **sun**. The sun provides energy for **producers** to grow.

Energy from the sun moves through a food chain when a living thing eats another living thing.

What is the process that producers use to turn energy from the sun into food?

producer

primary consumer

Primary consumers eat producers. Sea urchins are primary consumers. They love eating giant kelp!

Look back...

Which kingdoms make up the different parts of a food chain?

Secondary consumers eat primary consumers. In this case, sea otters eat sea urchins.

Sea otters are a *keystone* species. Find out what this means.

If you could add another arrow to this food chain, where would it go?

decomposer

Bacteria and fungi are **decomposers**. They break down dead organisms and turn them into nutrients. Plants use these nutrients (and the sun) to grow.

secondary consumer

tertiary consumer

Tertiary consumers eat the secondary consumers. Orcas are tertiary consumers. They eat sea otters and other animals.

Find one of the organisms from this food chain hidden in the unit.

 **STAGE 1**

- Research a different food chain. Draw it and label the living things with their names and roles.
- Think about how removing one living thing affects the food chain. Discuss with a partner.

If you remove … , … will …

HOW IS A FOOD WEB DIFFERENT FROM A FOOD CHAIN?

Discover...

the different relationships in a food web.

Most living things belong to more than one food chain.
Several food chains can be connected to make a **food web**.

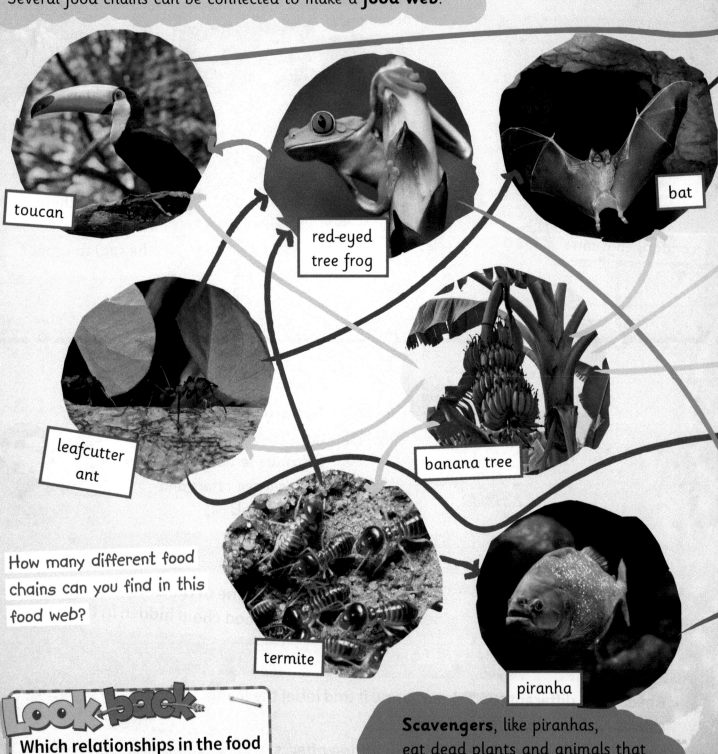

toucan

red-eyed tree frog

bat

leafcutter ant

banana tree

termite

piranha

How many different food chains can you find in this food web?

Look back...

Which relationships in the food web are competitive?

Scavengers, like piranhas, eat dead plants and animals that other living things kill.

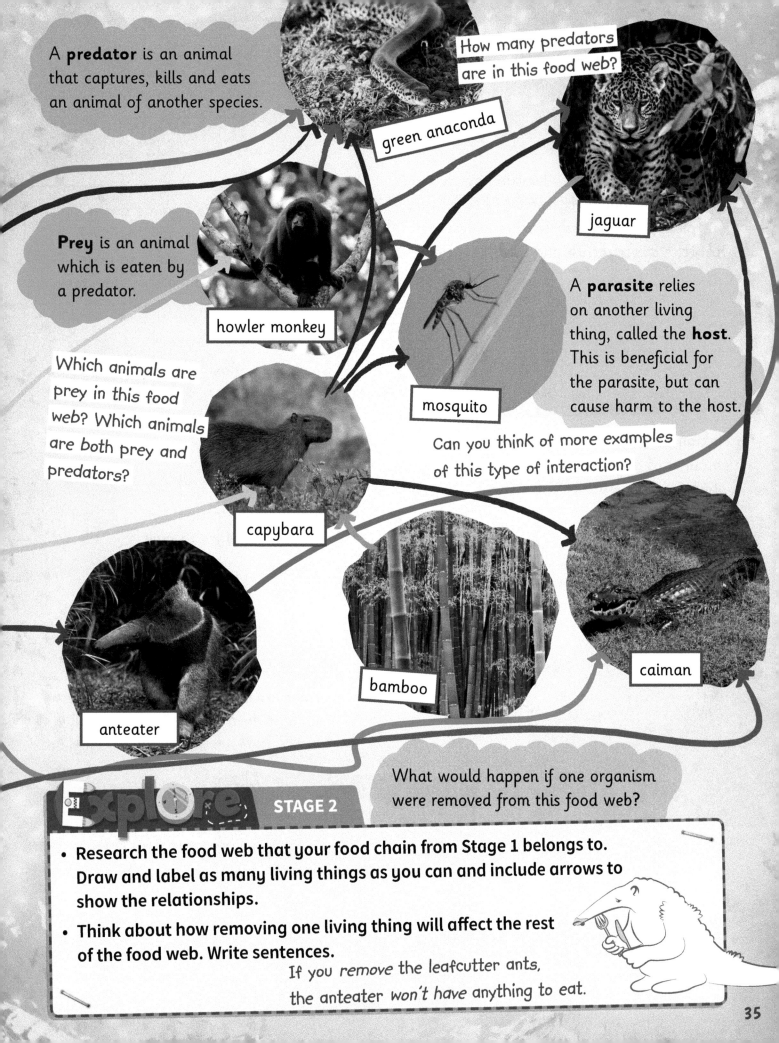

A **predator** is an animal that captures, kills and eats an animal of another species.

How many predators are in this food web?

green anaconda

jaguar

Prey is an animal which is eaten by a predator.

howler monkey

A **parasite** relies on another living thing, called the **host**. This is beneficial for the parasite, but can cause harm to the host.

mosquito

Which animals are prey in this food web? Which animals are both prey and predators?

Can you think of more examples of this type of interaction?

capybara

bamboo

caiman

anteater

What would happen if one organism were removed from this food web?

STAGE 2

- **Research the food web that your food chain from Stage 1 belongs to. Draw and label as many living things as you can and include arrows to show the relationships.**

- **Think about how removing one living thing will affect the rest of the food web. Write sentences.**

If you *remove* the leafcutter ants, the anteater *won't have* anything to eat.

WHAT CAUSES EXTINCTION?

Discover...

why global warming is such a threat to living things.

If a species disappears, this can have a huge impact on a food web. Instead of respecting our planet, humans are causing widespread **habitat destruction** and loss of species.

Listen to the programme about polar bears. Where do they live? How have they adapted to their habitat? What threats do they face?

Human activities produce large amounts of greenhouse gases, which increase **global warming**.

Global warming causes Arctic snow and ice to melt.

Global warming causes the temperature of the oceans to rise. Coral reefs are extremely sensitive to temperature change.

Deforestation, where large numbers of trees are cut down, is a major cause of habitat destruction. The land is then used for other purposes, mainly farming.

Find out more about how coral reefs are affected by global warming.

The Amazon rainforest produces 20% of the oxygen on Earth. What would happen if all the trees in the Amazon were cut down?

Cars and large factories cause **air** and **water** **pollution**.

Find out about an ecosystem that has been affected by this type of pollution.

As cities get larger, there is **less space** for living things to exist in their natural habitat.

Look back

Which species have adapted to living in cities?

Many species of animals are under threat due to **overfishing** and **overhunting**.

All of these changes can cause an entire species to die, resulting in **extinction**. As more and more species die out, there is **less biodiversity**.

Explore   STAGE 3

- Research the forms of habitat destruction that affect your food web. Which species do they affect?
- Discuss your research with a partner.

This food web is affected by …

This species will disappear if …

WHAT IS THE BEST WAY TO CLEAN UP AN OIL SPILL?

Find Out more...

Discover... how an oil spill spreads in the ocean.

Background: Oil spills affect all levels of an aquatic food web. They contaminate the water, making it too dirty to drink or live in.

Hypothesis: Which material or method is the best for cleaning up oil? Why?

Materials: plasticine, large container, water, toy animals, olive oil, washing up liquid, spoon, kitchen roll, sponge, cotton wool

Step 1: Recreate an oil spill. Line the edges of the container with plasticine to represent the shoreline. Add water and the toy animals. Pour some oil in the centre of the container.

Step 2: Try different materials and methods to clean up the oil.

Conclusion: What was the best way to clean up the oil?

The best way to clean up an oil spill is ...

... did not work as well as ...

It is better to ...

Reflect 1
What do you notice? What happens if the oil spreads to the shoreline?

Reflect 2
Which material or method is more effective? Why?

HOW CAN WE PROTECT SPECIES AND THEIR HABITATS?

Discover...

why biodiversity is important.

Nature reserves and **national parks** are special areas where certain activities, like fishing and hunting, are not permitted. Governments create them to protect wildlife and their habitats.

If a species is **endangered**, it is at risk of **extinction**. Many parks and reserves protect endangered species so that they do not die out.

Can you name these endangered species? Where do they live?

As responsible citizens, we must protect biodiversity. Biodiversity is important because all organisms are connected in the global ecosystem. When one organism is negatively affected, it can have negative effects on others as well.

Do you do any of these things? What other ways can you protect biodiversity?

Explore

STAGE 4

- Research a nature reserve. Where is it? What species does it protect? Why is the species under threat?

- Share your research with a partner. Listen and take notes.

1 **Complete the sentences in your notebook with *where, who, when* or *which*.**
  a Lions cooperate in family groups, ... are called prides.
  b Park rangers are people ..... work in national parks.
  c The rainforest is an ecosystem ..... plant species compete against each other for space and sunlight.
  d Vines are parasites ..... harm other plants by growing on them.
  e Predation occurs ..... a larger animal captures, kills and eats another animal.

2 **Complete the sentences. Use the example to help you.**
  a If you *remove* the sea otter from the food web, the sea urchin population *will increase*.
  b If we ..... (not / protect) endangered species, they ..... (become) extinct.
  c Global warming ..... (get worse) if we ..... (continue) burning fossil fuels.
  d If we ..... (act) as responsible citizens, we ..... (prevent) loss of biodiversity.
  e Many species ..... (disappear) if we ..... (not / stop) the deforestation of the rainforests.

3 **Read Jane's email about her trip to a national park. Write the correct answer for each gap. Write one word for each gap.**

> Hi Sally,
>
> I hope **(a)** ..... are well. Yesterday, we **(b)** ..... to the Norfolk Broads. It was an amazing day out! There was so **(c)** ..... to see and do. Did you **(d)** ..... that it's England's largest protected wetland? I saw lots **(e)** ..... animals, such as the Swallowtail, England's largest butterfly. I'll show you my photos **(f)** ..... I get back.
>
> See you soon,
>
> Jane

1 Look at the pictures. Unscramble the letters and write the words.

For more Unit 3 activities go to page 82.

a

b

c

d

o m t i t n i o c e p   i o n o p c e r a t o   r p r d u c e o   n m u c o s r e

2 Read the sentences. Choose the correct answer for each gap.

a The ..... includes all the ecosystems on Earth.

biosphere   flora   habitat

b The sun provides ..... with the energy they need to grow.

predators   producers   consumers

c It is necessary to have ..... to recycle organic material within ecosystems.

scavengers   hosts   decomposers

d ..... is when living things from the same species or different species work together.

Competition   Host   Cooperation

e Many ..... compete with each other for prey.

consumers   producers   decomposers

f We can all do a little each day to protect the Earth's ..... .

bioactivity   biology   biodiversity

FINALE

- In groups, plan the promotional material for your nature reserve.

- Decide on a name and location, what species it will protect and how. Include information on food chains, food webs and habitats.

  Help protect the beautiful ... !

- Make it attractive for people to visit.

  You can do your part by ...

Energy is all around us. It makes things happen and makes changes possible. Energy cannot be created or destroyed, but it can be changed from one form to another.

Look and discuss...

What forms of energy can you identify in the photos?

1

> This is ... energy because ...

> This also produces ... energy.

2

4

3

1 sound; 2 electrical / light; 3 chemical; 4 thermal / light; 5 electrical; 6 light; 7 kinetic / potential; 8 light / thermal

5

6

S ng
Forms of energy

7

What things can you see or hear working, moving or happening around you? This is energy!

8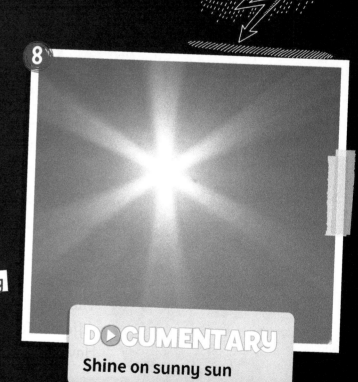

D CUMENTARY
Shine on sunny sun

Explore

Create a plan to save energy at home. You will:

- reflect on how you use energy.
- learn about using renewable and non-renewable energy.
- think about ways to save energy at home.
- convince your family to follow an energy-saving plan.

WHAT DIFFERENT FORMS OF ENERGY ARE THERE?

Energy exists in many forms.

Discover...

the relationship between potential, kinetic and mechanical energy.

Light energy is produced by the sun and is very important for the biosphere. There are other natural and artificial light sources, but the sun is the most important.

Can you give examples of other light sources?

Thermal energy, or **heat**, is the result of movement of tiny particles within an object. The faster they move, the more heat is generated.

Chemical energy is stored energy which is released when a chemical reaction takes place. The chemicals are broken down to produce a different form of energy. Are you feeling hungry? Have some tasty chemical energy. Yum!

Sound is energy made by vibrations. When an object vibrates, air particles around it vibrate too. This causes sound waves, which we can hear if they reach our ears.

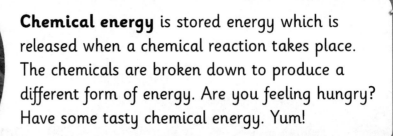

Electrical energy is used to power machines because it can be transformed into many different forms.

Potential energy is stored in objects. When this energy is released, it can do work.

Look at the dam. Where is the potential energy?

Kinetic energy is produced by movement. The heavier an object is and the faster it moves, the more kinetic energy it has got. Flowing water has got kinetic energy.

Mechanical energy is the sum of potential and kinetic energy that is used to do work. The **force** of the water moves the turbines. This is mechanical energy.

A bow and arrow is an example of mechanical energy. Explain why.

STAGE 1

- What forms of energy do you use every day? Make a list.
- Classify them according to when or where you use them: at home, at school or for hobbies.
- Make a class chart.

WHAT IS ENERGY TRANSFORMATION?

Discover...

what happens when wood burns.

We know that energy cannot be created or destroyed, but it can be changed. This is known as **transformation**.

When wood burns, **chemical energy** is transformed into **light** and **thermal energy**.

A toaster transforms **electrical energy** into **thermal energy**.

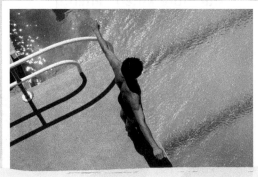

When you step off a diving board, **potential energy** is transformed into **kinetic energy** because of the pull of gravity.

Can you explain the energy transformations in this chain?

Find out what lost or wasted energy is.

 STAGE 2

- Look at the chart from Stage 1. Can you identify any energy transformations?
- Add them to the chart. Include any cases where energy is lost or wasted.

DO PLANTS NEED LIGHT TO GROW?

Discover... how plants react to different amounts of light.

Background: Producers transform light energy from the sun into chemical energy. They use this chemical energy to perform vital functions, such as growing.

Hypothesis: If a plant does not receive light energy, will it still be able to grow? Why / Why not?

Materials: two carrots, two plates, water, dark cupboard, ruler

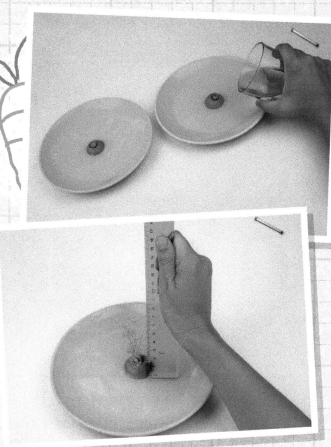

Step 1: Cut the top off each carrot and place it on a plate with water. Put one plate next to a window and the other in a dark cupboard.

Step 2: Wait seven days. Does a new stem grow from each carrot? If so, measure it.

Step 3: Keep measuring every day for one more week. It is important to water both plants.

Reflect 1 Which plant is the *control* experiment? Why?

Reflect 2 Which plant grows better?

This plant ... whereas this plant ...

Conclusion: How did the plant in the dark react without light energy? What about the plant by the window?

I can conclude ...

WHAT IS RENEWABLE ENERGY?

Energy exists in nature and can be changed into different forms for us to use. Some energy sources will never run out because they are **renewable**. Most of these do not cause pollution and are not harmful to the environment.

Find another machine that uses wind energy hidden in the unit.

Have you ever seen a wind farm? There are no animals! Instead, there are **turbines** which produce **mechanical energy**. This is then converted into **electrical energy.**

Solar energy is light from the sun. It can be transformed into electrical energy using **solar panels**.

The core of the Earth is extremely hot and some of the heat escapes to the surface. This is **geothermal energy**.

Investigate the uses of geothermal energy.

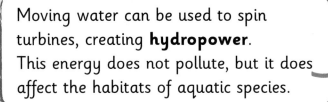

Biomass is a way to use trees, plants and rubbish to make energy.

Do you know how we get energy from biomass?

Moving water can be used to spin turbines, creating **hydropower**.
This energy does not pollute, but it does affect the habitats of aquatic species.

Try this ...

Does moving water have energy? Cut the top off a plastic bottle and punch six holes in the bottom. Put a short straw in each hole. Use three strings to hang the bottle and fill it with water. What happens?

Are there any disadvantages to using renewable energy sources?

Explore

STAGE 3

- Do you use any renewable energy at home or at school?
- How could you use renewable energy at home? Write down your ideas.

HOW WERE FOSSIL FUELS FORMED?

Discover...

how non-renewable energy sources can harm the environment.

Some natural energy sources are **non-renewable**. They cannot be replaced once they have been used up.

coal

oil

natural gas

Coal, oil and natural gas are **fossil fuels**.

Why are fossil fuels non-renewable?

1

2

Millions of years ago, the Earth was covered in swamps with giant ferns and trees.

3

There were also large oceans full of life.

4

As living things died, their bones settled on the ocean bed and in the swamps. They were covered with layers of sediment.

5

Over millions of years, under extreme pressure and heat, the decaying material turned into coal, oil or natural gas.

6

Now, we drill and mine to remove the Earth's reserve of fossil fuels.

Uranium is a non-renewable energy source that was formed millions of years ago. **Nuclear power stations** transform the chemical energy in uranium into electrical energy. Although uranium is non-renewable, we have enough to last for centuries.

How can these energy sources harm the environment?

The burning of fossil fuels contributes to global warming and causes **air pollution**. The pollution from power plants and factories rises into the atmosphere and falls as **acid rain**.

Find out how fossil fuels contribute to global warming.

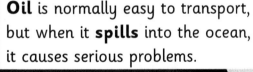

Oil is normally easy to transport, but when it **spills** into the ocean, it causes serious problems.

The biggest risk of using **nuclear power** is the **radioactive waste** it produces. It is dangerous when it is released into the environment and can cause cancer in humans.

How does polluted water affect food webs?

 **STAGE 4**

- Find out which non-renewable energy sources are used at home and at school.
- As a class, hold a debate discussing the best energy sources. Each group will represent a different energy source.

It's better to use ... because ...

I think ... would be better / more sustainable / more efficient.

Yes, but don't you think ... ?

1 🎧 **You will hear three short conversations. There is one question for each conversation. For each question, choose the correct photo.**

1 Which form of energy did Amy use at home?

2 What source of energy did the scientist, Marie Curie, research?

3 What problem is the town facing?

2 **Complete the sentences in your notebook. Use the example to help you.**

a If we *stop* burning fossil fuels, we *will decrease* global warming.

b Oil spills ..... (be) less common if we ..... (switch) to using renewable energy sources.

c If we ..... (reduce) our dependence on nuclear power, there ..... (be) less radioactive waste.

d If my school ..... (use) more renewable energy, ...

e If I ..... (save) energy, I ..... .

Content Review

1 Do the quiz! Are the sentences *true* or *false*? In teams, take turns answering. You get a bonus point for correcting any false statements. The team with the most points wins.

Assessment link

For more Unit 4 activities go to page 84.

Red Team

a Energy can be created, destroyed and transformed.

b Fossil fuels are renewable energy sources.

c The lighter an object is and the faster it moves, the more kinetic energy it has.

d When energy transformations are useful, we say the energy is lost or wasted.

e Burning fossil fuels can cause acid rain to fall.

f Although we may not notice, energy is all around us.

g There are some energy sources that will never run out because they are renewed continually.

Blue Team

a Radioactive waste is a big risk of using nuclear power.

b Oil, coal and natural gas are all forms of energy.

c We can use geothermal energy from the sun to do many things.

d Transforming chemical energy into electrical energy isn't useful to us.

e Energy is continually transformed.

f Energy makes changes and movement possible.

g When mechanical energy is released, it can do work.

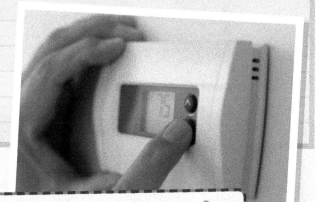

 **FINALE**

- Look back at all your information about energy use.
- Make a list of how your family could use less energy. Use the internet to research energy-saving techniques.
- Make a brochure, leaflet or calendar to show what everyone in your family should do.
- Encourage your family to follow your energy-saving plan at home.

We can save energy by …

If we save energy, we will …

SOUND, LIGHT AND HEAT

Look and discuss...

How do sound, light and heat energy travel? In what form? Look at the photos for clues.

Sound energy, light energy and heat energy can be found all around us. They have different properties and a few similarities.

1

2

3

Maybe they all travel in ...

Perhaps they move in ...

Sound, light and heat energy (from radiation) all move in waves, like the sea.

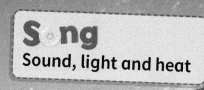

S♪ng
Sound, light and heat

In what ways are these forms of energy different? How are they similar?

How do you use sound, light and heat energy?

D▶CUMENTARY
Hear energy, see energy, feel energy

Explore!

Design a campaign warning people about the risks of too much energy. You will:
- learn about the risks related to different forms of energy: noise pollution, light pollution and excessive heat.
- investigate how to protect yourself against these risks.

IS THERE SOUND IN SPACE?

Discover...

how sound travels.

When an object **vibrates**, it produces **sound waves**. These waves travel through a medium (solid, liquid or gas) to our ears so that we can hear them.

We perceive large vibrations as **loud sounds** and small vibrations as **quiet sounds**.

Starting with the loudest, how would you order these sounds?

Sound waves can only travel through a medium, such as air. They cannot travel through a **vacuum**.

Sound moves four times faster through water than through air.

Can you explain why?

What is an echo? Which living things use echoes to navigate and hunt?

Space is a giant, empty vacuum with no air.

What a beautiful view!

Pardon?

Can sound travel in space? Why / why not?

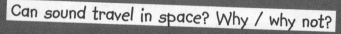 **STAGE 1**

- **What is the difference between *noise* and *sound*? Write definitions.**
- **What is noise pollution? What are its effects? Think about noise that bothers you.**
- **At home, open a window and listen for 10 minutes. Write down all the sounds you hear.**

Background: Cups and string can be used to make a simple telephone which shows how sound travels.

Hypothesis: What will happen if you change the length of the string? What will happen if you use a different material for the cord?

Materials: two plastic or paper cups, toothpick, scissors, string, paper clips, wool, sewing thread

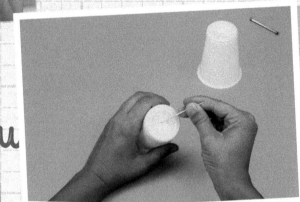

Step 1: Work in pairs. Make a hole in the bottom of each cup using a toothpick.

Step 2: Stand at opposite ends of the classroom. Talk into your cup using a normal voice. Your partner should hold their cup to their ear.

Step 3: Take a piece of string, put an end through the hole in each cup and attach it to a paper clip. Stand in the same places, pull the string tight and talk as before.

Reflect 1

Can you hear your partner? Why / why not?

Reflect 2

Can you hear your partner more clearly? What happens if you change the length of the string or use a different material?

Conclusion: Do the phones work better when they are connected? Why / why not? Does a shorter or longer piece of string work best? Why? Which material works best? Why?

... worked better because ...

The best material to use is ...

WHAT IS A LIGHT SOURCE?

Discover... the properties of light.

Light sources produce light energy. Without light energy, we wouldn't be able to see anything!

Light sources

artificial sources

natural sources

Artificial light sources are **man-made**. The light energy is **transformed** from another energy source, such as chemical energy or electrical energy.

Natural light sources are found in **nature**. The sun is the main source, but the Northern Lights are also natural.

Can you name more light sources for each category?

The moon reflects the light from the sun. It looks as if it is shining, but is it a light source?

These plankton produce their own light. This is called *bioluminescence*. Is this light natural or artificial? Which other living things produce their own light?

Speed

Find out how long it takes for light to travel from the sun to the Earth.

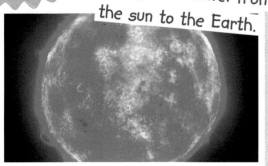

Sound travels quickly, but not as fast as light. Light travels at about **300,000 kilometres per second**. This is called the **speed of light**.

Direction

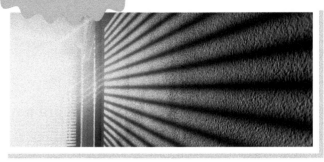

Like sound, light energy travels in waves. However, unlike sound, light energy travels in **straight lines**, called **rays**.

Light energy does not need to travel through a medium and it cannot pass through all materials.

Colour

What do the words *translucent*, *transparent* and *opaque* mean?

Humans can only see a very small amount of **visible light**. This light appears white to us, but it is really made up of all colours.

When light comes into contact with an object, the light can be **absorbed**, **reflected** or **refracted**.

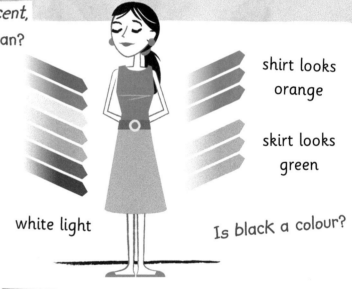

shirt looks orange

skirt looks green

white light

Is black a colour?

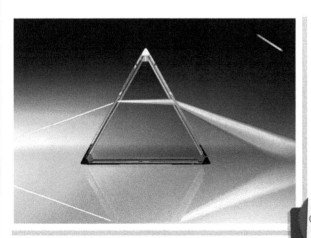

Explore · STAGE 2

- **What is light pollution? What causes it?**
- **Is there light pollution where you live?**
- **What are the effects of light pollution? Find out!**

Look back

How do plants use light energy?

HOW DOES A SUBMARINE SEE ABOVE WATER?

Discover...

which surfaces reflect light the best.

Reflection occurs when rays of light are not absorbed by an object and bounce off, instead.

smooth surface

rough surface

Light **reflects** in the same direction on smooth surfaces. On rough surfaces, it reflects in all directions.

Lots of different surfaces reflect light.

Mirrors are smooth, shiny surfaces that reflect light very well. They reflect the object in front of them.

Submarines use mirrors in a **periscope** to see what is happening above the water.

Try this ...

Investigate how a periscope works. You will need a laser pen and two small mirrors.

We use mirrors in lots of other places too!

Dentists use mirrors to see our teeth.

What other jobs use mirrors?

HOW ARE RAINBOWS FORMED?

Discover...

what refraction is.

Light travels in a straight line, but when it passes through a medium with a different **density**, it changes direction. This is called **refraction**.

Find the rainbow-coloured object hidden in the unit.

A rainbow is caused by refraction. When sunlight hits water droplets in the air, the light **refracts**. The different colours in white light bend at different angles and are separated, so we see the seven colours.

We use refraction to help us see. Lots of everyday objects use **lenses**, which are pieces of curved plastic or glass. These refract the light and can make objects look bigger or smaller.

What objects can you name that use a lens?

Try this...

HELLO

Water is very dense and refracts light very well. When we place a word behind a glass of water, how will the word look? Write down your hypothesis, then test it out!

Explore   STAGE 3

- How can sunlight be harmful to our skin? Find out!
- Record the information you have learnt about the negative effects of light in a chart.
- Add the information about sound.

cause	effect	prevention

WHAT IS THE DIFFERENCE BETWEEN HEAT AND TEMPERATURE?

Discover...

what thermal conductors and insulators are.

Heat is thermal energy, which can be transferred from molecules with **high** thermal energy to molecules with **low** thermal energy.

Heat can travel in any direction, but it always flows from hot to cold.

Heat and temperature are related, but not the same. **Temperature** measures how hot or cold something is. The higher the temperature, the faster the molecules move.

Heat is energy. Temperature is a measure of the energy.

Electrical energy and chemical energy can be transformed into heat energy. These are **artificial heat sources**.

How many artificial heat sources can you name?

Life on Earth would not exist without the heat from the sun. It is a **natural heat source**. We also get heat from inside the Earth, called **geothermal energy**.

What other natural heat sources do you know?

Listen to two pupils talking. What is a thermal conductor? What is a thermal insulator? Give an example of each.

WHAT IS EVAPORATION?

Heat can change the **state of matter**.

When solids like butter and ice are heated, they become liquids. This is called **melting**.

Try this...

When liquid water is heated, it turns into a gas. This is called **evaporation**.

Can you explain what happened and why?

What happens to air when it is heated? Stretch a balloon over the mouth of an empty bottle and fill a bowl with hot water. Before you stand the bottle in the bowl, write down your hypothesis. What do you think will happen?

How does a hot air balloon work?

As matter is heated, it will expand or get bigger (but you can't always see this happening!). The molecules move around more and at a faster rate. This is called **expansion**.

What happens to an object when it is cooled?

Explore   STAGE 4

- Investigate the negative effects related to heat: burns, heat exhaustion and heat stroke.
- How can we prevent these conditions?
- Add the information to your chart from Stage 3.

1 **Complete the sentences in your notebook. Use the example to help you.**

a Sound energy *is produced* when you play the piano.

b Light ..... (refract) by a lens to make an object appear bigger or smaller.

c When a substance ..... (heat), its molecules move around more and at a faster rate.

d When you turn on a lamp, electrical energy ..... (transform) into light energy.

e Geothermal energy ..... (generate) inside the Earth.

2 **What *will* or *won't* happen? Complete the sentences.**

Heat changes the state of matter. What **(a)** ..... happen if different objects are heated? When a gas, like air, is heated, it **(b)** ..... contract; it **(c)** ..... expand. When a liquid, like water, is heated, it **(d)** ..... evaporate. When a solid is heated, like chocolate, it **(e)** ..... melt very quickly!

3 **With a partner, talk about the forms of energy in each photo.**
Use *used to* and *didn't use to*.

a

b

✔Assessment link

For more Unit 5 activities go to page 86.

1 Read the sentences below and choose the correct word for each space.

a ..... travels in a straight line.

Sound   Heat   Light

b Sound waves must travel through a ..... .

medium   vacuum   surface

c When light hits a ..... surface, it reflects in all directions.

smooth   rough   coloured

d Light cannot pass through objects that are

transparent   opaque   translucent

e ..... changes the state of matter.

Sound   Heat   Light

f ..... is when a liquid changes to a gas.

Melting   Expansion   Evaporation

2 Draw pictures to illustrate the main properties of light. Include reflection and refraction. Label your drawings.

Explore   **FINALE**

- Choose either sound, light or heat energy. Create a campaign to warn against the negative effects of being exposed to too much energy.

- Invent a slogan, choose images and make up a short and catchy chant.

- Present your ideas to the class. As a class, vote for the best campaign.

6 ELECTRICITY

We all use electricity every day. Can you imagine your day without any electricity? Think about all these machines. How would you carry out daily tasks without electricity?

Look and discuss...

Can you name the machines?
Which ones do you use every day?

I use a ... every day because ...

I need a ... to ...

1 washing machine; 2 oven; 3 fridge; 4 toaster; 5 microwave; 6 dishwasher; 7 television; 8 lamp; 9 laptop; 10 mobile phone; 11 hairdryer

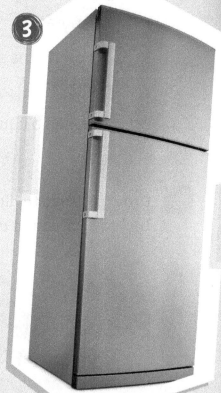

What energy transformations can you identify?

Explore

Design and build a light-up board game. You will:
- learn about static and current electricity.
- learn about and build an electrical circuit.
- research famous inventors and their inventions.

D▶CUMENTARY
Electricity everywhere

WHAT IS ELECTRICITY?

Discover...

the different particles that make up an atom.

Electricity is a type of **energy**. To understand how it works, we need to understand atoms!

If you rub two objects together, **electrons can move** from one atom to another, which makes the objects electrically charged.

All matter is made up of **atoms**. They have a structure like this.

Build an atom model with different coloured plasticine.

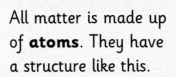

In the **nucleus**, there are **protons**, with a positive electric charge, and **neutrons**, with no electric charge. **Electrons**, with a negative electric charge, move around outside the nucleus.

An atom is **electrically neutral** when it has the same number of protons and electrons.

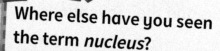

Look back

Where else have you seen the term *nucleus*?

68

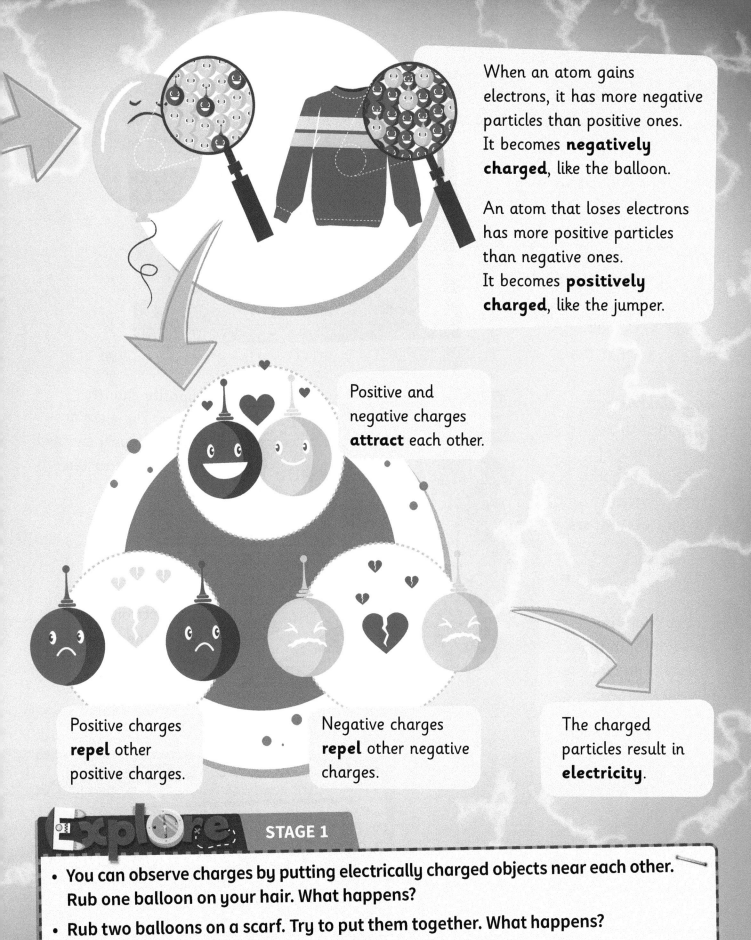

When an atom gains electrons, it has more negative particles than positive ones. It becomes **negatively charged**, like the balloon.

An atom that loses electrons has more positive particles than negative ones. It becomes **positively charged**, like the jumper.

Positive and negative charges **attract** each other.

Positive charges **repel** other positive charges.

Negative charges **repel** other negative charges.

The charged particles result in **electricity**.

STAGE 1

- You can observe charges by putting electrically charged objects near each other. Rub one balloon on your hair. What happens?
- Rub two balloons on a scarf. Try to put them together. What happens?
- Draw a diagram to explain.

WHAT CAUSES LIGHTNING?

Electricity can build up in one place, or flow from one place to another. When electricity gathers in one place, it is known as **static electricity.**

What do we call electricity that flows?

Static electricity occurs when there is an imbalance of positive and negative charges between two **electrical insulators**.

Electrons from the boy rub off onto the carpet, leaving him positively charged.

Opposite charges attract. The electrons of a negatively charged object are attracted to a positively charged object.

When lots of electrons move at the same time, you might see a spark or feel a small shock.

Lightning is caused by static electricity.

Rain clouds move very fast. The water, air and ice particles rub against each other and create a static electrical charge.

When the charge is big enough, the clouds release the energy, which we see as lightning.

What other types of energy are released in an electrical storm?

HOW DOES CURRENT ELECTRICITY WORK?

Discover... the different components of an electrical circuit.

Not all electricity is static. Electricity that flows is called **current electricity**. It occurs when electrons are passed quickly from one atom to another within certain materials.

conductor

insulator

Good **electrical conductors**, like wires and other metal objects, allow electricity to travel through them easily. **Electrical insulators**, such as rubber, plastic and wood do not allow electricity to pass through them.

An **electrical circuit** allows electrons to flow through a path.

Find another electrical insulator hidden in the unit.

Switch: this opens and closes the circuit and can stop the flow of electricity.

Power source: this provides the electrical energy. A battery is a power source.

Electricity from a power source travels through a circuit and is transformed into another type of useful energy.

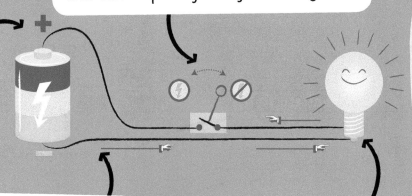

Wires: these conduct electricity.

Resistor: this transforms electricity into other forms of energy. A lightbulb is a resistor.

STAGE 2

- Think about how to create an electrical circuit with the following: 3.5V lightbulb, 4.5V battery, insulated copper wire and a switch.
- Draw a plan of the circuit.
- Build your circuit. Make sure the lightbulb works!

HOW DO EXTRA LIGHTBULBS AFFECT A CIRCUIT?

Discover... _what voltage is._

Background: Batteries give off a specific amount of electrical energy or power. This is measured in voltage. If a lightbulb reads 3.5 Volts, that means it needs a battery that provides at least 3.5 Volts of electrical energy.

Hypothesis: What will happen if you add another lightbulb to a circuit? What will happen to the lightbulb if you add another battery?

Materials: two 3.5V lightbulbs, two 4.5V batteries, insulated copper wire, switch

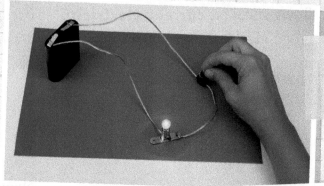

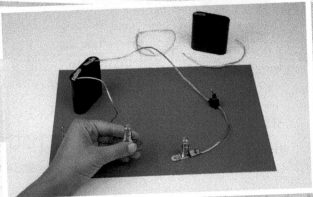

Step 1: Build the circuit from page 71. Take note of how bright the light is.

Step 2: Disconnect the wire between the lightbulb and the battery. Add another lightbulb between these two components and then connect the circuit again.

Step 3: Now add a second battery to the circuit and reconnect the circuit.

Step 4: Completely disconnect the second lightbulb from the circuit, but leave both batteries attached. Reconnect the circuit.

Reflect 1
What do you notice about the light from each lightbulb?

Reflect 2
Is there any change in the light?

Reflect 3
What happens to the lightbulb?

Conclusion: Describe what happens when you make changes to the components in a circuit. Why do these changes happen?

Adding an additional ... makes the light brighter / dimmer.

This happens because ...

WHO WAS THOMAS EDISON?

Discover... some of the inventions patented by Edison.

Thomas Edison was a famous American inventor. He was born in 1847. He patented over 1,000 inventions.

Edison's most famous contribution was the **lightbulb**. Before this, people used candles and oil lamps, which were smoky and messy.

What energy transformation occurs in a lightbulb?

Thomas Edison was a hard worker and very hopeful. He also believed that you should always keep trying for a solution.

> I have not failed. I've just found 10,000 ways that won't work.

> Genius is one percent inspiration and ninety-nine percent perspiration.

Listen to find out more about Thomas Edison and his inventions. Write down the key information you hear.

Explore

STAGE 3

- Research some other famous inventors. Find out about their inventions and when they invented them. Use the internet to help you.

- Use your research to make matching cards. Match inventors to inventions, or inventions to dates. Remember to include Edison!

lightbulb

Thomas Edison

1879

73

CAN YOU NAME THESE INVENTIONS?

Discover...

some famous inventions and their inventors.

An **invention** is the creation of a new device, process or product. Inventions can make our lives easier and safer.

How? Talk with your partner and give examples.

1 8 7 9

Inventor:
Thomas Edison

Invention:
Lightbulb

Function:
It transforms electrical energy into light energy.

1 8 0 0

Inventor:
Alessandro Volta

Invention: **Battery**

Function:
It transforms chemical energy into electrical energy.

1 8 3 1

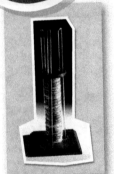

Inventor:
Michael Faraday

Invention:
Electrical generator

Function:
It transforms mechanical energy into electrical energy.

1 8 7 6

Inventor:
Alexander Graham Bell

Invention:
Telephone

Function:
It allows people to communicate quickly and over long distances.

1888

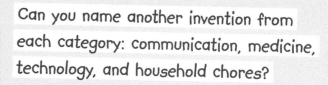

Can you name another invention from each category: communication, medicine, technology, and household chores?

Inventor:
Nikola Tesla

Invention:
Alternating current motor

Function:
It allows electricity to travel longer distances through power lines, decreasing the number of power stations needed.

1936

Inventor:
Alan Turing

Invention:
Computer

Function:
It processes information, and shows it on a screen.

1894

Computers used to take up an entire room. Nowadays, people can fit them in their pockets!

Inventor:
Guglielmo Marconi

Invention: **Radio transmitter**

Function:
It transmits sound over air instead of through wires.

Explore　　　STAGE 4

- Add these inventors and inventions to the cards you prepared in Stage 3.
- Now design a board game using the matching cards.
- Think about how you could include an electrical circuit to make your game more interesting.
- Draw a plan of your game in your notebook.

1 **Complete the sentences in your notebook with the correct tag questions.**

a You know all about being safe around electricity, ... ?

b She's a qualified electrician, ... ?

c You unplugged the toaster before cleaning it, ... ?

d You didn't touch the light switch with wet hands, ... ?

e He hasn't been flying his kite near a power line, ... ?

f They weren't being unsafe around electricity, ... ?

2 **Complete the sentences by transforming the verbs *invent* or *discover*.**

a The telephone is considered a very important ..... because it enabled us to communicate quicker and over long distances.

b Christopher Columbus, an Italian ..... , landed in America in 1492.

c Fire was an important ..... for humans.

d Thomas Edison is a famous American ..... .

e Benjamin Franklin, an American scientist, ... electric charges.

f It was Alessandro Volta who ..... the battery in 1800.

3 **Read this email from your English-speaking friend, Sam, and write a reply. Write 100 words.**

From: Sam

To: .....

Hi!

We're learning about important machines in Science class. Do you know any? Who invented them? Where can I get more information?

Looking forward to hearing from you.

Sam

1 Are the sentences *true* or *false*?
Correct the false sentences.

 **Assessment link**

For more Unit 6 activities go to page 88.

a Not many machines use electricity.

b All matter is made up of atoms, even the chair you are sitting on!

c Static electricity flows through a circuit.

d Lightning is an example of current electricity.

e Alexander Graham Bell invented the lightbulb and the telephone.

f An electrical circuit allows electrons to flow through a closed path along wires.

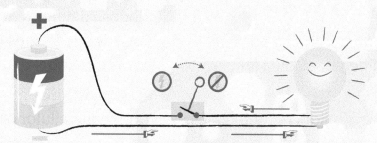

2 Match the vocabulary with the definitions.

a A material that allows energy to flow easily.

b The part of an atom with a negative electric charge.

c The flow of charge through a material.

d When an atom has the same number of protons and electrons.

electrically neutral

electrical current

electron

electrical conductor

Explore FINALE

- Now make your board game, using the plan you created in Stage 4.

- If you can, try to include an electrical circuit.

- Get into groups and play your board games. Who knows the most about inventors and their inventions? Who designed the best board game?

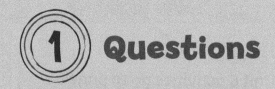

Questions

1   Name the characteristics that define all living things.

2   Make up a chant with a friend to remember the main structures in a cell and their function.

3   Draw and label a plant cell and an animal cell. Use different colours for the structures.

4   Different cells share similar characteristics. Name four things common to all cells.

5   What have plant cells got that animal cells haven't?

6   Why are cells known as *the building blocks of life*?

7   List the different levels of organisation that make up an organism.

8   Choose a human organ system. What organs and tissues make up this system? Draw and label a diagram.

9   Explain the difference between unicellular and multicellular organisms.

10 Name one organism from each of the five kingdoms that might be found in your local park.

1   An icicle can grow, but is it living? Why or why not?

2   Can cells survive without a nucleus? Find out what these cells are called.

3   All plant cells contain chloroplasts. How do these provide energy for the cell?

4   Why is it important for a cell to be specific about what it lets in?

5   Imagine you are a cell. Write a short story about your life. Where are you located? What do you do?

6   A giant sequoia tree has a circumference of 3,130 cm. The average child has an arm length of 122 cm. How many children need to hold hands to circle the tree?

7   We eat mushrooms and they look a lot like plants. Why are they not in the Plant Kingdom?

8   Type 1 diabetes affects cells in the pancreas that produce insulin, which regulates the body's sugar. Insulin has an impact on blood vessels, nerves, the heart, eyes and kidneys. What levels of organisation does the disease affect?

9   Unicellular fungi, called yeast, play a major role in our diet. Find out more about yeast in our diet.

10 Use the internet to list organisms from each of the five kingdoms that live near the beach.

Study aid

START

What's the difference between a plant and animal cell?

Name the structures in an animal cell.

MOVE AHEAD 2 SPACES

Why are plants so rigid?

Name a tissue in your bones.

How do scientists classify unknown organisms?

MOVE BACK 3 SPACES

Guess a strange animal your partner describes.

What are the five kingdoms?

What are organs made up of?

MOVE AHEAD 3 SPACES

What is the Monera kingdom?

Describe a protist.

Name a system in your body.

How are animals classified?

MOVE BACK 3 SPACES

To win the game, name the 7 characteristics of all living things.

YOU WIN!

Tip

Play a board game to revise content. Roll a die and move your counter to a circle. If you answer the question incorrectly, go back to the start!

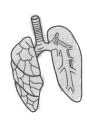

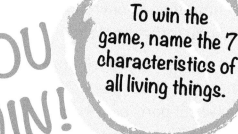

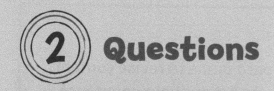

(2) Questions

Think about it

1. What is an ecosystem? What components make up an ecosystem?

2. Name the abiotic factors that influence an ecosystem.

3. Name the living and non-living things from one of the ecosystems you studied.

4. Draw examples of an individual, a population and a community.

5. If there are 500,000 bacteria in 1 ml of puddle water, how many bacteria are there in 5 litres? Is this an example of a community or a population?

6. How have organisms adapted to living in the desert?

7. Draw a forest ecosystem. List the living and non-living elements in a chart.

8. Which ecosystem includes coral reefs? List some animals that live in coral reefs.

9. Which animals have adapted to living in urban ecosystems?

10. Create and draw your own ecosystem. Describe it to a classmate. What are the natural and artificial elements?

Think harder

1. Choose an ecosystem. What would happen if you removed or changed one abiotic factor?

2. Make up a song about the living and non-living things in one of the ecosystems you studied.

3. Find out about the great wildebeest migration. What dangers do the wildebeest face?

4. In the grasslands, prey animals are either well camouflaged or very fast. Which would you rather be? Why?

5. Why is the health of the Amazon rainforest so important to our planet? What happens when we cut parts of it down?

6. What adaptations has the Fennec fox got to keep cool in the desert?

7. Imagine you are going to the North Pole. What would you do to prepare for the long, cold journey? Write a journal entry.

8. Planet Earth is 70% water. Make a chart to show the amounts of the different types of water and where this water occurs.

9. What type of ecosystem is a puddle? It is natural or artificial? Why can the organisms survive in such a small ecosystem?

10. Research a recent ecocatastrophe and its effects on the environment.

Study aid

Tip

Use a table to summarise key information. Copy and complete the table in your notebook to help you organise all the information you learnt about the different ecosystems. Take turns describing each one with a friend.

Ecosystem	Type	Picture	Abiotic Factors	Flora	Fauna
Grassland	Temperate		Cool climates, dry (not much rain), soil	Different types of short grass	Iberian lynx, bison, deer, wolves, rabbits
	Savannah		Always warm, not enough water for trees, soil	Different types of long grass	Elephants giraffes, zebras, lions, rhinos
Desert					

Questions

1 What is the biosphere? Write a definition.

2 Give an example of an interaction between species which demonstrates cooperation.

3 Draw a food chain using real examples. Connect the links and label the different parts.

4 What are the differences between primary, secondary and tertiary consumers?

5 What role do decomposers play in a food chain?

6 Name a prey-predator relationship. What adaptations does each animal have for catching prey / avoiding being caught?

7 Besides predators and prey, list other ways living things interact in a food web.

8 Name five ways that humans destroy the habitats of other living things.

9 What is a nature reserve? Name and describe a nature reserve that exists in Spain.

10 We are spending time in the biosphere whenever we are outdoors! Write to a pen pal describing your favourite outdoor activity.

1 Would a pride of lions be affected if a drought caused most of the grass to die? Why?

2 Research and give examples of the following relationships: mutualism and commensalism.

3 Investigate the threats facing sea otters, a keystone species. How might these affect the food chain?

4 Research a bear's diet. Are they primary, secondary or tertiary consumers? Why do they eat such a variety of things?

5 What would happen if there were no decomposers?

6 Describe what happens to the number of predators when the number of prey increases.

7 Are parasites important in a food web? What might happen if we removed all the mosquitos from the rainforest food web?

8 Design a poster advertising the negative effects of human impacts on biodiversity.

9 Why is it important to create and maintain nature reserves and national parks?

10 Imagine your favourite outdoor place was damaged. How would you feel? Write a letter to an adult asking for help to protect your favourite outdoor place.

Study aid

Tip

Graphic organisers are great for organising information. Choose a different ecosystem. Draw the graphic organiser and place the organisms from that ecosystem in the correct layers.

decomposers

tertiary consumers

secondary consumers

primary consumers

producers

Questions

Think about it

1. Name all the forms of energy in your classroom.

2. Which forms of energy are in: a hamburger; a light bulb; a moving bicycle; a guitar?

3. Choose a form of energy from question 1. Where did the energy come from? Is energy transformation occurring?

4. List all the renewable energy sources you know. What forms of energy do they produce?

5. What energy transformations take place within a modern wind turbine?

6. What are the differences between non-renewable and renewable energy sources?

7. Write five *true* or *false* statements about energy. Pair up and discuss the statements.

8. Name and describe the types of pollution caused by non-renewable energy use.

9. Why is it important for humans to use less non-renewable energy sources?

10. Write down what your family does to save energy at home. How could they save more energy?

Think harder

1. Imagine a day without electrical energy. How would it change your daily routine?

2. What forms of energy are used to make a birthday cake? Think about the ingredients, the mixing, the baking and the eating.

3. Describe the energy transformations taking place when you kick a football.

4. It could take up to 4,000 years for a rainforest to grow back naturally. Why might wood from the rainforest not be a renewable resource?

5. What are the similarities and differences between windmills from the past and modern wind turbines?

6. Imagine you are on the town council and have to decide whether to build a nuclear power plant or a wind farm. Which would you choose? Why?

7. Write five quiz questions about non-renewable resources. Ask and answer in pairs.

8. Smog is a combination of smoke and fog. Research the effects of smog on the peppered moths in England in the 1800s.

9. What is sustainable development? How would you develop a city to maximise this?

10. Find out how your hometown or city plans to save energy and protect the environment.

Study aid

Tip

Use a list of pros and cons to evaluate information. Choose two different energy sources and make a list of their pros and cons.

Coal

Pros
- Cheap compared to other energy sources.
- Abundant energy source (compared to oil and gas).
- Produces large quantities of energy when burnt.
- Electricity produced from burning coal is reliable.
- Not dependent on the weather.

Cons
- Non-renewable energy; it will run out eventually.
- Produces large quantities of carbon dioxide and other harmful gases when burnt.
- Contributes to global warming, causes air pollution and acid rain.
- Expensive to transport.
- Coal mining destroys the landscape and is dangerous for people working in the mines.

Wind energy

Pros
- Renewable energy; it will never run out.
- Does not pollute the environment.
- Wind turbines are space efficient.
- Wind farms are relatively cheap to build.
- No mining or transportation costs.

Cons
- Dependent on weather; wind does not blow reliably.
- Good wind sites are often remote and far away from where the electricity is needed.
- Can harm wildlife such as birds.
- Wind turbines cause noise pollution.
- Some people think wind farms are ugly and spoil the landscape.

Questions

1. What are the properties of sound? Explain why there is no sound in space.

2. Onomatopoeia is a word that makes a sound, like *hiss, bang* or *chirp*. List some more examples.

3. Name two artificial light sources and two natural light sources. How are they different?

4. What happens when light comes into contact with an object? Does it always behave in the same way? Explain.

5. What is the difference between reflection and refraction? Name an example of each.

6. Is the moon a light source? Explain.

7. Which energy sources produce both light and heat?

8. True or false? The lower the temperature of an object, the greater its thermal energy. Explain.

9. What is the difference between a thermal insulator and a thermal conductor?

10. How does heat affect the following: chocolate; ice cream; water; ice; metal? Draw diagrams to illustrate your answers.

1. Describe how you hear the sound produced by a guitar. Draw a diagram.

2. Imagine you lost your hearing for a day. What would the day be like? Write a journal entry.

3. How can we reduce the negative effects of light pollution?

4. Discuss with a partner: Light refracts when it hits an object.

5. Describe what happens when light passes through a prism.

6. Find out more about bioluminescence. How do organisms produce this type of light?

7. Find out how light and heat contribute to the greenhouse effect. Draw a diagram and explain it to a partner

8. Draw a diagram of an ice cream melting. In what direction does the thermal energy flow? Why? Repeat the activity with a bowl of hot soup.

9. If we want a block of ice to melt faster, why would wrapping it in a blanket be a bad idea?

10. You had a really fun birthday party last night, but when you woke up, all the balloons were smaller and had fallen to the ground. Explain why.

Study aid

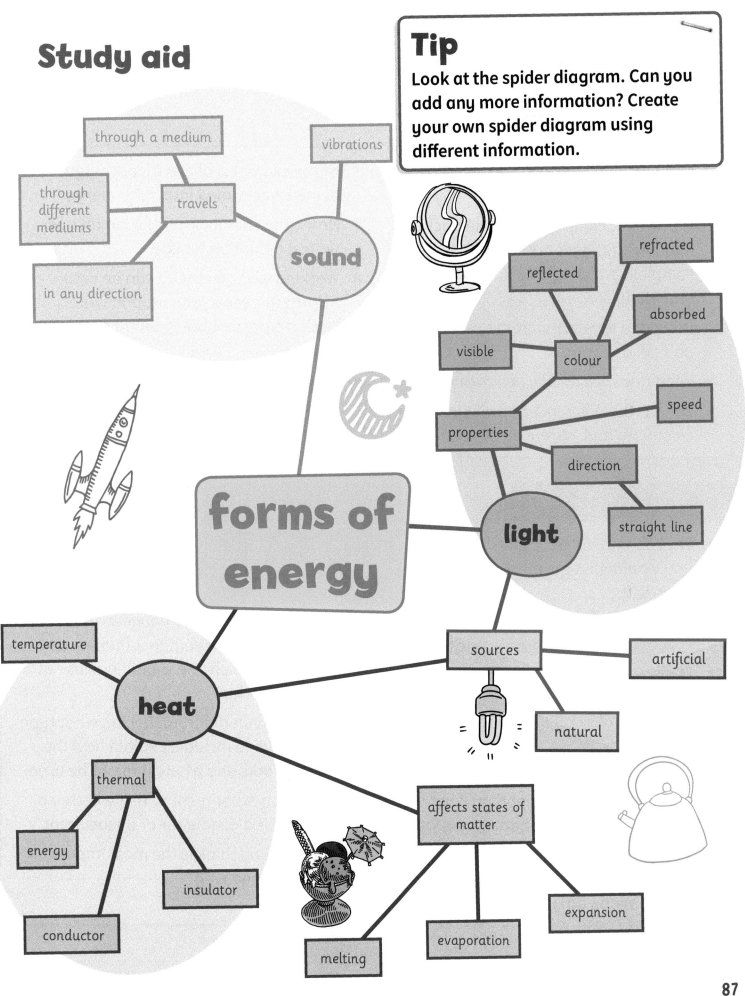

Tip
Look at the spider diagram. Can you add any more information? Create your own spider diagram using different information.

through a medium

through different mediums — travels — vibrations

in any direction

sound

reflected

refracted

visible — colour — absorbed

properties — speed

direction

straight line

light

forms of energy

temperature

heat — sources — artificial

thermal

energy

insulator

conductor

natural

affects states of matter

melting

evaporation

expansion

87

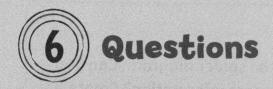

6 Questions

Think about it

1 Write down all the ways you have used electricity today.

2 Name a machine that uses electricity and one that does not. Which one is more complex? Which one do you use more in your daily life?

3 Draw and label a diagram to show the parts of an atom.

4 What does *electrically neutral* mean?

5 What is the difference between static electricity and current electricity?

6 Name examples of electrical energy being transformed into light energy.

7 Name the components of a circuit and write a definition for each.

8 Working with electricity can be very hazardous, especially around water. Design a poster about electrical safety.

9 Most electronics and appliances use wires made of copper wrapped in plastic. Why?

10 Draw a famous invention. Add some information about the inventor.

Think harder

1 Write to a friend about the three things you would miss the most if there was no electricity.

2 Keep an electricity journal for one week. How could you use less electricity?

3 Many machines nowadays are wireless and portable. How do they get their electricity?

4 Draw a diagram of a negatively charged and a positively charged atom interacting with one another. What would a diagram look like if both atoms were positively charged?

5 Describe what is happening when you rub a balloon on your hair.

6 Why doesn't electricity flow through an electrical circuit when the switch is turned off?

7 What is the difference between the Edison lightbulb and the compact fluorescent lightbulb? Which one should you use at home and why?

8 Draw a circuit diagram. Decide what type of resistors to include. Explain how the circuit works and where it might be used.

9 Design an experiment to test whether a material is a conductor or an insulator.

10 What do you think is the most important invention and why?

Study aid

Tip

What other information could you add to the graphic organiser about electricity? Create a similar organiser using different content you have studied.

static electricity

- Builds up in one place.
- Caused by an imbalance of charges.

current electricity

- Flows from one place to another.
- Powers many devices in our homes.

electricity

charge

- Atoms with more electrons than protons are negatively charged.
- Negative charges repel other negative charges.

machines and devices

- The lightbulb – Thomas Edison
- The computer – Alan Turing

1 Organise your studying

Make a flap book to study the levels of organisation and classification.

Materials: two sheets of A4 card, pencil, ruler, stapler, scissors, colouring materials, white paper (optional)

Step 1: Divide one sheet of card into 10 squares with a ruler and pencil. Staple it to the other sheet along both long edges.

Step 2: Only cutting the top sheet, cut along the centre line. Then cut along the other lines to make five flaps on each side.

Step 3: Draw a level of body organisation (cell, tissue, organ, system, individual) on the five left flaps.

Step 4: Draw an organism from each of the five kingdoms (Monera, Protist, Fungi, Plant, Animal) on the five right flaps.

Step 5: Under each flap, write the characteristics of the structure or organism.

2 Ecosystems in 3D

Choose an ecosystem and make a three-dimensional book.

Materials: A4 card, scissors, glue, colouring materials, photos of organisms from your ecosystem

Step 1: Cut three or four sheets of A4 card in half horizontally (to make size A5). Cut one of the A5 sheets in half again. These two smaller pieces will connect the book.

Step 2: Draw the background of your ecosystem on one of the A5 sheets.

Step 3: On the other A5 sheets, draw a border around the outside. Decorate the borders with pictures of organisms from your ecosystem.

Step 4: Cut along the borders to make windows on the pages.

Step 5: Decide on the order of your pages, putting the background last. Make sure you can see all the organisms!

Step 6: Fold the two smaller pieces of card like an accordion. Glue each border page to an inner fold. Your 3D book is ready!

3 What's for dinner?

Choose a food chain and make a collage. Who eats who?

Materials: A4 card, pencil, colouring materials, scissors, glue, creative materials to decorate, string

Step 1: Plan your food chain. Decide how to represent each link in the food chain.

Step 2: Draw the tertiary consumer. It should cover a whole sheet of A4 card and have a big, open mouth!

Step 3: Draw the rest of the links in the food chain on other sheets of card. Each one should be a little smaller so it fits inside the mouth of the previous link. Don't forget to include the sun.

Step 4: Use creative materials to decorate each link, like tissue paper, felt or foam.

Step 5: Glue your food chain links one inside the other.

Step 6: Make a decomposer. Attach it with a piece of string so it can be placed between any link.

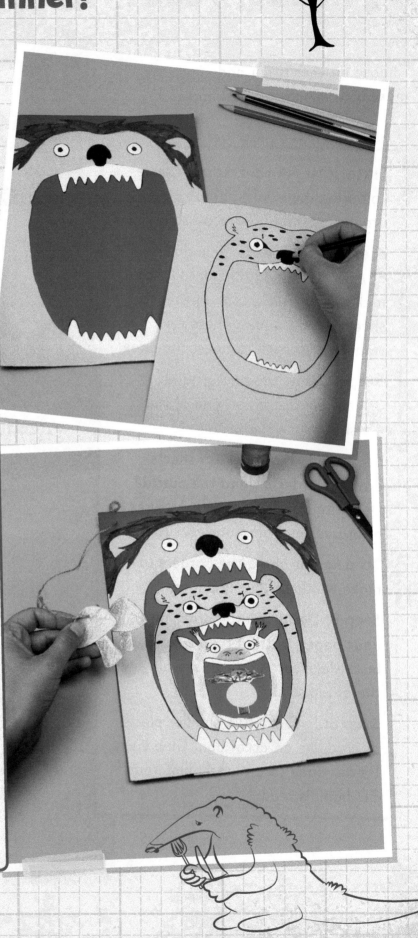

4 Cooking with the sun

Make a solar oven to warm pizza, toast marshmallows or melt chocolate.

Materials: cardboard box, marker, ruler, scissors, aluminium foil, glue, plastic wrap, tape, black paper, food to warm

Step 1: Draw a square on the box lid, about 2 cm from the edge. Cut out three sides and fold the flap back along the uncut edge. Glue aluminium foil to the underside of the flap.

Step 2: Cut two pieces of plastic wrap the same size as the box lid. Open the box and tape the plastic inside in a double layer over the hole. Make sure the edges are sealed.

Step 3: Inside the box, glue a piece of aluminium foil to the bottom, then sheets of black paper on top.

Step 4: Place the box in direct sunlight with the food inside. Prop open the flap at an angle that allows the most sunlight into the box.

⑤ Jumping for science

Using your body heat, make a coin jump on the top of a bottle.

Materials: coin, glass bottle, bowl of cold water with ice in it

Step 1: Place the coin and neck of the glass bottle into the bowl of icy water for 10 minutes.

Step 2: Do the next steps quickly. Place the bottle on a table. Place the coin on the mouth of the bottle. Wrap your warm hands around the bottle and wait.

Observations: Does anything happen to the coin? Why? If not, leave the bottle in the icy water for longer.

Extension: What other experiments can you think of to show heat expansion?

6 Machines in steps

Remember, you can transform one form of energy into another!

Rube Goldberg was a cartoonist and engineer best known for his wacky inventions. Design and create a machine that works in steps.

Step 1: Look up different Rube Goldberg machines on the internet. Some are very complex, but others are simple.

Step 2: Plan a machine in your notebook. What do you want it to do: ring a bell, make a toy car move, turn on a lightbulb? Think of three or four steps to make it happen and draw them.

Step 3: Think of the best materials for each step. Now, build your machine.

Step 4: To make the machine do what you want, you may have to try different methods and materials!

The machine will work over and over again, just reset it and show your friends!

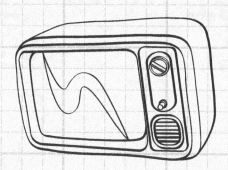

Acknowledgements

The authors and publishers acknowledge the following sources of copyright material and are grateful for the permissions granted. While every effort has been made, it has not always been possible to identify the sources of all the material used, or to trace all copyright holders. If any omissions are brought to our notice, we will be happy to include the appropriate acknowledgements on reprinting and in the next update to the digital edition, as applicable.

Photo acknowledgements

All images are sourced from Getty Images.

p. 3, p. 6: Keren Su/Stone; p. 4: IMAGEMORE Co., Ltd., Elena Yurchenko/EyeEm, GoodLifeStudio/iStock/Getty Images Plus, Paul Bradbury/OJO Images, Phil Boorman/Cultura, Steve Kaufman/Corbis Documentary, sturti/E+, Squaredpixels/E; p. 4, p. 61, p. 65: Hero Images; pp. 4–5: FUMIO OKITA/amana images; p. 5: AllAGRI/iStock/Getty Images Plus, p. 5, p. 11, p. 33, p. 37, p. 49, p. 58, p. 83, p. 93: saemilee/DigitalVision Vectors; p. 6: Edwin Godinho/EyeEm, Kidsada Manchinda, Roland Birke/Photographer's Choice, DEA/G. WRIGHT/De Agostini Picture Library, paule858/E+, Travelpix Ltd/Stone, Keren Su/Stone; p. 6, p. 28, p. 35, p. 83: Danita Delimont/Gallo Images; pp. 6–7: Navapon_Plodprong/iStock; p. 8, p. 12, p. 79: Nnehring/E+; pp. 8–9, pp. 24–25, pp. 38–39, pp. 46–47, pp. 56–57, pp. 72–73, pp. 90–95: novaaleksandra/iStock/Getty Images Plus; p. 9: Andy Ryan, znm/Mauritius; p. 11, p. 79: Andrew_Howe/E+; p. 11: Monsterstock1/iStock/Getty Images Plus, tunart/E+ p. 11: kamil/iStock, BSIP/Universal Images Group, yenwen/E+, jamtoons/DigitalVision Vectors, LokFung/DigitalVision Vectors; p. 11, p. 14, p. 37, p. 60: LokFung/DigitalVision Vectors; p. 12: Reinhard Dirscherl/WaterFrame, Richard Cummins/Lonely Planet Images; p. 12, p. 83: JESPER KLAUSEN/Science Photo Library; p. 13, p. 29, p. 83: Arterra/Contributor/Universal Images Group; p. 13: agustavop/iStock/Getty Images Plus, Weimann/Oxford Scientific, scrambler27/RooM, Satirus/iStock/Getty Images Plus, Peter Purdy/Stringer/Hulton; p. 14, p. 90: quantum_orange/DigitalVision Vectors; p. 14, p. 43, p. 46, p. 63, p. 65, p. 67, p. 75, p. 85, p. 87, p. 89, p. 90, p. 94: FrankRamspott/DigitalVision Vectors; p. 14: Dorling Kindersley; p. 15: Auscape, protechpr/iStock/Getty Images Plus, James Gerholdt/Photolibrary, Susan Davies/EyeEm; p. 15, p. 19, p. 81: Daniela Dirscherl/WaterFrame; pp. 16–17: Aleksandar Reba/EyeEm; p. 16: SCIEPRO/Science Photo Library, Science Photo Library; p. 18: Anton Petrus, hadynyah/E+, mstwin/iStock/Getty Images Plus, Geography Photos/Universal Images Group; p. 18, p. 19, p. 41, p. 91: Vect0r0vich/iStock/Getty Images Plus; p. 19: Andres Garcia Martin/iStock Editorial/Getty Images Plus; p. 19, p. 52: Westend61; p. 19, p. 91: carlacdesign/iStock/Getty Images Plus; pp. 18–19: kenpixl/E+; p. 20: Gregory_DUBUS/iStock/Getty Images Plus, aniszewski/iStock; p. 20, p. 39, p. 41, p. 81, p. 83, p. 92: topform84/iStock/Getty Images Plus; p. 21: Richard Kemp/Oxford Scientific, VanWyckExpress/E+, zhouyousifang, Georgette Douwma/The Image Bank; p. 22, p. 81: 1001slide/iStock/Getty Images Plus; p. 22, p. 81: Lunnderboy/iStock/Getty Images Plus; p. 22: Daniel Hernanz Ramos/Moment; p. 23: Marcus Siebert/imageBROKER, Gisela Delpho/Picture Press, Wolfgang Kaehler/LightRocket, Olena_Znak/iStock/Getty Images Plus; p. 25: Wayne Lynch/All Canada Photos, Jami Tarris/The Image Bank, richcarey/iStock/Getty Images Plus; p. 26: Reinhard Dirscherl/WaterFrame/Corbis Documentary, Steve Terrill/Corbis, Philippe-Alexandre Chevallier/Biosphoto, Andrew McLachlan/All Canada Photos; p. 27: JGI/Daniel Grill/Blend Images, Geslin/Nature Picture Library; pp. 28–29: Brandon Tabiolo/Perspectives; p. 28: Peter Unge/Lonely Planet Images, Philippe Lissac/Corbis Documentary; p. 29, p. 81: ©Juan Carlos Vindas/Moment; p. 30: Steve Allen/The Image Bank, Ignacio Palacios, AndreAnita, jez_bennett; p. 31: WIN-Initiative, Ann & Steve Toon/robertharding, Tammy616, millerpd; pp. 30–31: Peter Zelei Images/Moment; p. 32: bgfoto, Ralph A. Clevenger, Joe Dovala/WaterFrame; p. 33: David Courtenay, John Hyde, Franco Banfi/WaterFrame, hchjjl/iStock/Getty Images Plus; p. 34, p. 83: Marka/Universal Images Group; p. 34, p. 83: Johner Images; p. 34, p. 35, p. 83: webguzs/iStock/Getty Images Plus; p. 34, p. 83: swisshippo; p. 34, p. 83: Snowleopard1/Vetta; p. 34, p. 83: The best pictures come from a sincere heart/Moment Open; p. 34: User10095428_393/iStock/Getty Images Plus; p. 35, p. 83: inoc/Moment; p. 35, p. 83: Gabrielle Therin-Weise/Photographer's Choice RF; p. 35, p. 83: Tom Brakefield/Corbis Documentary; p. 35: icon72/iStock/Getty Images Plus; p. 35, p. 83: Panoramic Images; p. 35: Sven Zacek; p. 36: acilo/E+, Jenny E. Ross/Corbis Documentary, Jones/Shimlock–Secret Sea Visions/Oxford Scientific, shaunl/E+; p. 37: Toa55/iStock/Getty Images Plus, Amanda Hall/robertharding, Jeffrey Rotman/Corbis Documentary, Morkel Erasmus, Carsten Krieger/Nature Picture Library, Maria_Galybina/iStock/Getty Images Plus; p. 38: Matthew D White/Photolibrary, Win McNamee/Staff/Getty Images News; p. 39:

PobladuraFCG/iStock/Getty Images Plus, KenCanning/E+, Hira Punjabi, MyLoupe/Universal Images Group, KidStock/Blend Images, Steve Sparrow/Cultura; pp. 40–41: Erik Avent/EyeEm; p. 40: Alys Tomlinson/Cultura, simonlong/Moment; p. 41: Krijn Trimbos/naturepl.com/Nature Picture Library, Canon_Bob/iStock/Getty Images Plus, Liesel Bockl, Corbis Documentary, Michael DeYoung/Perspectives; pp. 42–43: Sabrina Bekeschus Monteiro/EyeEm; p. 42: Imgorthand/E+, Jon Edwards/Photolibrary, Yamaki Yuri/EyeEm, daniel reiter/Moment; p. 43: Sami Sarkis/Photographer's Choice, Skyhobo/E+, Bruno Ehrs/Corbis Documentary; p. 44: Sigit Nugroho/EyeEm, deepblue4you/E+, Peter Dazeley/Photographer's Choice, claudio.arnese/E+; p. 45, p. 46: Maskot, Blake Little/The Image Bank; p. 46: Jörg Mikus/EyeEm, Tuan Tran/Moment, Chris Ryan/OJO Images, Ingram Publishing, Wuthipong Pangjai/EyeEm, Daria Botieva/Eyeem, DarthArt/iStock/Getty Images Plus; p. 47: ANATOLII MIKHAILOV/FOAP; p. 48, p. 85: David Wall Photo/Lonely Planet Images; p. 48: republica/iStock/Getty Images Plus, Peerakit Jirachetthakun; p. 49: ConstantinosZ/iStock/Getty Images Plus, Visage/Stockbyte; p. 50, p. 85: Monty Rakusen/Cultura; p. 50: morkeman/Vetta, yesfoto/E+; p. 51: abadonian/iStock/Getty Images Plus, Schroptschop/E+, PETER PARKS/AFP, Will & Deni McIntyre/Corbis Documentary, PIERRE-PHILIPPE MARCOU/Stringer/AFP, Creativemarc/iStock/Getty Images Plus, AFP/Stringerv; pp. 52–53: Spencer Baker/EyeEm; p. 52: eggeeggjiew/iStock/Getty Images Plus, deepblue4you/iStock/Getty Images Plus, PeteWill/E+, Martin Diebel, bjdlzx/iStock/Getty Images Plus, Ludwig Werle/Picture Press, Martin Harvey/Corbis Documentary, DuKai photographer/Moment; p. 53: Tetra Images; pp. 54–55: David Pu'u; p. 54: Dougal Waters/DigitalVision, Sean Malyon/Cultura, www.fredconcha.com/Moment; p. 55: Drazen/iStock/Getty Images Plus, Heath Korvola/DigitalVision, ucius/iStock; p. 56: Les Stocker, Karl Weatherly, Webeye/E+, Stuart Westmorland/Corbis Documentary, 1971yes/iStock/Getty Images Plus; p. 56, p. 87: ONYXprj/iStock/Getty Images Plus; p. 57: nyul/iStock/Getty Images Plus, asiseeit/E+; p. 58: Arctic-Images/Stone, ampcool22/iStock/Getty Images Plus, Julia Davila-Lampe/Moment, Doug Perrine/Nature Picture Library, bulentozber; p. 58, p. 73, p. 89: owattaphotos/iStock/Getty Images Plus; p. 59: Science Photo Library – SCIEPRO, Thomas M. Scheer/EyeEm, Ian Cuming/Ikon Images, Lam Yik Fei/Stringer; p. 60: nattrass, BananaStock, Dimitri Otis/Photographer's Choice, Jeff Overs/BBC News & Current Affairs; p. 61: Andy Crawford/Dorling Kindersley p. 61: mikroman6/Moment; p. 62: stocknroll/iStock/Getty Images Plus, Peter Unger/Lonely Planet Images, Adam Crowley/Blend Images, kokouu/iStock/Getty Images Plus; p. 63: Datacraft Co Ltd, JanPietruszka/iStock, Astronaut Images/Caiaimage, Kevin T. Levesque/Lonely Planet Images, cat_arch_angel/iStock/Getty Images Plus; pp. 64–65: Daniel A. Leifheit/Moment; p. 64: Kirn Vintage Stock/Corbis Historical, Bohunka Zemanova/EyeEm, Lumi Images/Alexandra Dost, Moritz Haisch/EyeEm; p. 65: Rubberball/Mike Kemp; pp. 66–67: Ryan McVay/Photodisc; pp. 66: s-cphoto/E+, vblinov/iStock/Getty Images Plus, Grassetto/iStock/Getty Images Plus; p. 66, p. 67: bonetta/iStock/Getty Images Plus; p. 67: dashadima/iStock/Getty Images Plus, Andy Crawford/Dorling Kindersley, omada/iStock/Getty Images Plus, alexsl/iStock/Getty Images Plus, ppart/iStock/Getty Images Plus; p. 70: David Frazier/The Image Bank, Wild Horizon/Universal Images Group; p. 71: istmylisa/iStock/Getty Images Plus, 5second/iStock/Getty Images Plus; p. 73: Education Images/UIG/Universal Images Group, choness/iStock/Gsetty Images Plus; p. 73, p. 74, p. 75: Science & Society Picture Library; p. 74: ZU_09/E+, Royal Institution/SSPL, Apic/Hulton Archive, Stock Montage/Archive Photos, Universal History Archive/Universal Images Group, Bettmann, Chris Hunter/Corbis Historical, Print Collector/Hulton Archive, p. 74, p. 95: etse1112/iStock/Getty Images Plus; p. 75: John Parrot/Stocktrek Images, Heritage Images/Hulton Archive, Creative Crop/Photodisc, Arkadivna/iStock/Getty Images Plus; pp. 76–77: Image Source; p. 76: Flavio Edreira/EyeEm, Ritesh Dadhich/EyeEm; p. 77: YolandaVanNiekerk/iStock/Getty Images Plus, p. 77: Andersen Ross/Blend Images; p. 79: Magnilion/DigitalVision Vectors; p. 87: ourlifelooklikeballoon/iStock/Getty Images Plus; p. 89: saw/DigitalVision Vectors; p. 91: carlacdesign/iStock/Getty Images Plus; p. 93: ilyast/DigitalVision Vectors; p. 95: Jeffrey Coolidge/Stone p. 95: Boston Globe.

Front cover photography by Eric Isselee/Shutterstock, Vitaly Korovin/Shutterstock, gopause/Shutterstock, pedrosala/Shutterstock, Raimundo79/Shutterstock, Africa Studio/Shutterstock, Chansom Pantip/Shutterstock, studiovin/Shutterstock, Ortis/Shutterstock, Zamurovic/Shutterstock, Chansom Pantip/Shutterstock, Csanad Kiss/Shutterstock, Venus Kaewyoo/Shutterstock.

Designer: Chefer

The authors and publishers would like to thank the following illustrators:
Kay Coenen (Advocate Art) pp 8, 10, 24, 56 (tr), 59, 60 (t), 62, 65 (t), 68, 69, 71, 77, 79; Dave Smith (Beehive Illustration) pp 45, 49, 50, 60 (bl), 61, 63 (cr), 70.